Whatever is Lovely

A 40-DAY DEVOTIONAL THROUGH THE GARDEN

PHOTOS & DEVOTIONALS BY

Janet Allgood

WHATEVER IS LOVELY—A 40-DAY DEVOTIONAL THROUGH THE GARDEN

Published by Janet Allgood | Burlington, Iowa

Prepared for Publication: www.palmtreeproductions.com

ISBN (Paperback): 979-8-9873538-0-6

ISBN (Hardcase): 979-8-9873538-1-3

Printed in the United States of America

Follow the author—

 janet_allgood

 Janet Allgood

THIS BOOK IS PRESENTED TO
BY

acknowledgments

All these photos were captured at the beautiful
Crapo Park in Burlington, Iowa.

I wish to say thank you to the city of Burlington for creating such a lovely space for the public to enjoy and to the skilled workers who so diligently cultivate the gardens and tend to the grounds—preserving the natural beauty of every season.

foreword

It has been such a delight to have a front row seat to this labor of love. Everything contained in this book is simply an overflow of Janet's heart. In a season when many have been searching for answers, I have seen my wife's life message come into sharp focus, "To point others to the goodness of God, the beauty of creation, and the glory He has placed in each of us." And that is what this project has been all about.

Many mornings I have watched Janet leave the house with great anticipation—hoping to capture the perfect photo with her newest lens. But, the greatest gift she brings to this devotional is how vividly she sees through the lenses of her Father's eyes. Every day I see her undone by the beauty and wonder and joy of the creation all around us. This book is more than a collection of pretty pictures and inspiring thoughts. It is an impartation of grace from a life that has been forever changed by the GOODNESS and GLORY of God.

JEFF ALLGOOD

introduction

You are invited to join me on a walk through the park. On our stroll, we will find ever-changing beauty, refreshing stillness, and a world of possibilities. It is a perfect place to reflect and meet with God. Every time we meditate on His Word, we have an opportunity to encounter the Author of Life. It is then we discover that everything which is good and lovely comes from Him.

lovely—having qualities that inspire love, affection, or admiration;
beautiful, exquisite;
graceful, spiritually pleasing

Finally, brothers and sisters, whatever is true, whatever is noble, whatever is right, whatever is pure, whatever is lovely, whatever is admirable—if anything is excellent or praiseworthy—think about such things.

PHILIPPIANS 4:8

beauty

—qualities in a person or thing that evoke pleasure or satisfaction, something that delights the senses or mind.

Our journey begins with the promise of a new spring. It is a transitional time of year when the temperature has warmed enough for magnolia blossoms to begin emerging—but winter has not fully loosened its grip. Each year in the Midwest, our hearts long for the hope of spring and the new life that emerges from the earth. So, when a late snowfall appears, it would be easy to grumble in disappointment. However, if you are on a journey to discover the beauty and goodness God has placed in every moment… you embrace it!

You walk outdoors, lift your gaze heavenward and feel each snowflake alight on your face. You are captivated by the intricate beauty and uniqueness of a snowflake nestled on your sleeve. Then you pause long enough to be engulfed in the surround sound of stillness blanketing the atmosphere. That's when gratitude begins to well up in your heart, and you start to see more than what meets the eye. God gives you a fresh revelation as you realize all of your senses are pointing back to your Creator. Then you know without a doubt: This is my Father's house. He creates beauty out of love for me!

The four corners of the earth were formed by your hands, and
every changing season owes its beauty to You.

PSALM 74:17

Thank you, Lord, for your infinite creativity and the beauty of every changing season. My heart is refreshed in You.

gentleness

—the quality of being kind and tender; having a calm, soft and soothing nature.

The Star Magnolia is one of the forerunners in the spring parade of flowering trees. Its pale pink blossoms daintily unfold from velvety buds in only a few hours. As if being adorned in an elegant pink robe, the scene feels soft and light. I see the gentleness of the Father as I gaze upon the pastel serenity of the scene. And I hear His still, small voice as He invites me to draw near.

From the creation of the world, the invisible qualities of God's nature have been made visible, such as his eternal power and transcendence. He has made his wonderful attributes easily perceived, for seeing the visible makes us understand the invisible.

ROMANS 1:20

Images are a part of our heart language. What we behold with our eyes can bring illumination to our spirit. The blossoming Star Magnolia provides a fitting display of gentleness. It is a character quality we find in God that is safe, warm, and inviting.

Jesus said, "Come to Me, all who are weary and burdened, and I will give you rest. Take My yoke upon you and learn from Me, for I am gentle and humble in heart."

MATTHEW 11:28-29.

Lord, thank You for your gentleness—that tender aspect of Your character which invites me to draw near, breathe deeply, and find rest in You.

joy

—a feeling of exhilaration or delight; a state of happiness and contentment; experiencing the fulfillment of a deep desire/longing.

Over just a few short days, the soft pink blossoms of the Star Magnolia are transformed into a gala of white petals—ushering in a celebration of spring! What a privilege it is to gaze upon such a dazzling work and be stirred by the delight of the Master Artist. It makes me giddy with laughter! God is the most joyful being in the universe. It is an amazing attribute of our Heavenly Father, and He loves to share it with His children.

You make known to me the path of life; You will fill me with joy in your presence, with eternal pleasures at Your right hand.

PSALM 16:11

The joy of the Lord is your strength.

NEHEMIAH 8:10

Splendor and majesty are before Him; strength and joy are in His dwelling place.

1 CHRONICLES 16:27

There is no doubt that God's creation was designed to bring us great joy. But an even greater reality is that the Lord Himself is joy! Where He is present, there is joy. Scripture goes on to remind us that "the joy of the Lord is our strength." It's difficult for my finite mind to wrap itself around this remarkable truth. There is a powerful relationship between the joy of the Lord and the strength He provides. The sweet thing is, we don't have to figure it all out—we just get to live in it!

Thank you, Lord, that You are JOY. You love to create things that bring us joy and fill our hearts with rejoicing! You are a loving Heavenly Father who invites us to find the fulfillment of our deepest longing in You.

3

—the anticipation of something good; confident expectation.

Hope is the joyful anticipation that God's GOODNESS will come through. It is the atmosphere that fuels our faith. Increased hope is simply a byproduct of seeing God more clearly. And true hope is never based on our circumstances.

God uses the canvas of spring to paint a breathtaking picture of resurrection and new life. Daffodils are one of the first flowers to spring forth from the lifeless ground as heralds of a new season. They are a lovely and captivating picture of new beginnings. You cannot look at a garden of brilliant daffodils gazing up at the sun as they sway gracefully in the breeze and not be filled with hope!

Praise be to the God and Father of our Lord Jesus Christ! In His great mercy, He has given us new birth into a living hope through the resurrection of Jesus Christ from the dead, and into an inheritance that can never perish, spoil or fade—kept in heaven for you.

1 PETER 1:3-4

So as a gift of His love, since we are faultless—innocent before His face—we can now become heirs of all things, all because of an overflowing hope of eternal life.

TITUS 3:7 TPT

Jesus, You rose from the dead to give us new life! You make all things new. May we live each day in the hope and mighty power of Your resurrection! Thank You for the promise of spring—for new life and fresh beginnings. We are forever grateful for what You have done. You are our living hope.

—unwavering belief; complete trust; firm confidence.

Our faith is anchored in three things—1) an unwavering belief in God that is not shaken by our senses or our circumstances, 2) a complete trust in our Father's goodness and love, 3) and a firm confidence that the Lord will always come through—not one of His promises will fall to the ground.

Consider how wildflowers grow freely without any intervention from human hands. There is a sense of wonder and joyful surprise when coming upon a patch of wildflowers in bloom. It's as if the Master Designer drew from his palette—providing just the right highlights and splashes of color to His work. To witness these blossoms thriving, despite never being tended by a person, makes their existence especially delightful and mysterious.

Our faith is a bit like a wildflower. We don't know where it comes from. We can't see our Father as He creates, plants, and tends to our faith. He sows in our hearts a deep longing to know Him—to encounter the very source of life. He is the author and perfecter of our faith.

The fundamental fact of existence is that this trust in God, this faith, is the firm foundation under everything that makes life worth living.

HEBREWS 11:1 MSG

The next time you come upon Dutchman's Britches—unique strands of blossoms that grow freely in the woods—be reminded that they are there by God's design. And if He puts that much care into the wildflowers, consider His delight in fashioning you!

Thank You, Lord, for our faith. It is with firm confidence we can "Be sure of what we hope for and certain of what we do not see" (Hebrews 11:1).

5

—a conscious choice not to be driven by self-interest or pride,
but to focus on the value and needs of others

Oh, the sweet and humble Bluebell! Without a hint of self-importance, its delicate pink buds transform into regal blue flowers that gracefully bow in honor to their Creator. Each spring, its blooms faithfully return to carpet the woodland gardens.

It is in Jesus that we find a picture of true humility—fueled by a heart overflowing with love. The Master showed us what it looks like to lead like a servant and serve like a King. He lived a life completely yielded to the Father. Then, in the ultimate sacrifice, Jesus laid down His life in order to set us free.

Take My yoke upon you and learn from Me, for I am gentle and humble in heart.

MATTHEW 11:29

Do nothing out of selfish ambition or vain conceit.
Rather, in humility, value others above yourselves.

PHILIPPIANS 2:3

And being found in appearance as a man, He humbled himself and became obedient to death—even death on a cross! Therefore God exalted Him to the highest place and gave Him the name that is above every name …

PHILIPPIANS 2:8-9

Oh, what a Savior! I bow down in humble adoration.

destiny

—something that is to happen; a predetermined course of events.

The vibrant pink blossoms of the Flowering Crab tree grace the landscape in early spring. The views are stunningly beautiful! Every branch, every petal is a reflection of the Lord's attention to detail. All of creation provides testimony that there is a plan and a purpose to everything under Heaven.

Can you not discern this new day of destiny breaking forth around you? The early signs of My purposes and plans are bursting forth. The budding vines of new life are now blooming every-where. The fragrance of flowers whispers, "There is change in the air..."

SONG OF SONGS 2:13 TPT

For I know the plans I have for you," declares the Lord, "plans to prosper you and not to harm you, plans to give you hope and a future."

JEREMIAH 29:11

God has a special plan and purpose for each of His children. But, for many this has felt like a bleak time, lacking in fruitfulness. Yet, God has been purposeful about preparing soil and strengthening roots for the season ahead. Can you discern your destiny breaking forth? By faith and prayer it is time to lay ahold of the hope and the future that God has in store for you!

Thank You, Lord, for the assurance that You have a plan and purpose for my life. I am humbled that You would choose me and walk on this life journey with me. And I am amazed how You take my dreams and my destiny, and weave them into something beautiful.

experiential knowledge

—personal familiarity through encounter, perception and discovery that leads to increased awareness and understanding.

Words cannot adequately express the experience of sitting under a brilliant white canopy of blossoms on a clear spring day. There is a gentle breeze blowing, a robin sings a happy tune, the sunlight sparkles as it filters through the delicate petals and fragrance fills the air. The atmosphere can only be described as heavenly. Throughout nature we encounter a knowledge of the glory of the Lord.

The heavens declare the glory of God; the skies proclaim the work of his hands.
Day after day they pour forth speech; night after night they display knowledge.
There is no speech or language where their voice is not heard …

PSALM 19:1-4

Everything we could ever need for life and complete devotion to God has already been deposited in us by His divine power. For all this was lavished upon us through the rich experience of knowing Him who has called us by name …

2 PETER 1:3 TPT

Conventional knowledge fills our mind with information. Experiential knowledge leads to transformation. The head ponders facts, but the heart pursues faith. The study of Scripture is essential to becoming grounded in the truth of who God is and how He has called us to live. But, it is not enough to know about God. Our spirit and all of our senses are tuned to encounter God, and truly know the Lord of love.

I pray that you, being rooted and established in love, may have power, together with all the Lord's holy people, to grasp how wide and long and high and deep is the love of Christ, and to know this love that surpasses knowledge— that you may be filled to the measure of all the fullness of God.

EPHESIANS 3:17B-19

8

Meditate on Psalm 19:1-4 and think of a time when creation spoke to you without a sound … and you knew with all of your heart—God is glorious and His creativity knows no bounds! Now invite Him into a fresh encounter. Ask the Lord to reveal to you more of Himself, His purposes, and His ways.

—to express approval or admiration; to celebrate or proclaim someone's character or achievements.

The Dogwood tree comes into bloom around the same time as the Flowering Crabapple, serving up a feast for the eyes—a festival of color! I am fascinated by the way each blossom gracefully sways in the breeze while pointing heavenward—as if joining in a song of praise to the God of creation!

I'm thanking you, God, from a full heart, I'm writing the book on Your wonders,
I'm whistling, laughing, and jumping for joy; I'm singing Your song, High God.

PSALM 9:1-2 MSG

The reason I love this verse so much is because God has brought me into a season where I am living in it. A thankful heart and eyes of wonder are a gateway into His presence. And in His presence there is fullness of joy!

You can pass through His open gates with the password of praise. Come right into His presence with thanksgiving. Come bring your thank offering to Him and affectionately bless His beautiful name!

PSALM 100:4 TPT

It started by admiring the beauty I could see with my eyes. But, what filled my heart with praise was a deeper affection for the One who envisioned the splendor of a Dogwood in bloom—then spoke it into existence. "For seeing the visible makes us understand the invisible ..." Romans 1:20

I'm singing Your song, High God ... I'm bursting with praise for who You are, and all You have done—and I want the world to know!

wisdom

—the capacity to make sound decisions based on knowledge, experience and judgment; the ability to recognize the best course of action.

It was only recently that I became aware of a unique woodland plant—the Mayapple. I'm not sure how I missed it for so long, and now it seems easy to recognize. Its generous twin leaves unfurl into a showy umbrella which provides a canopy of shade to a solitary, exquisite white blossom. In the summer, each flower produces a single yellow-green fruit. This wild perennial is typically found in wooded colonies—with all the plants arising from one root.

Wisdom is seeing with divine perspective. It is a gift that the Father loves to give to all His children who seek it. Wisdom grows from a life rooted in the Word, and abiding in the shadow of the Most High. Much like the Mayapple blossom, it reveals treasure hidden in plain sight.

If any of you lacks wisdom, you should ask God, who gives generously to all without finding fault, and it will be given to you.

JAMES 1:5

I know that You delight to set Your truth deep in my spirit. So come into the hidden places of my heart and teach me wisdom.

PSALM 51:6 TPT

Father, give me a discerning heart of wisdom: To know what You would say, and to do what You would do. By your Spirit, lead me into all truth. May wisdom blossom in my life, yielding the fruit of creativity, beauty and excellence—causing the world to gaze upon Your glory! Amen.

—to experience great pleasure or satisfaction; a stirring of the senses that evokes joy

This little beauty is a Red Trillium. It is native to the eastern half of the U.S. and blooms in early spring. Its crimson form brings a touch of elegance and nobility to the shaded woodlands. The Trillium is appropriately named for the three lush petals of its solitary flower. The diamond-shaped leaves gracefully whorl around the stem like a ballerina in mid-pirouette.

Great are the works of the Lord; they are pondered by all who delight in them.

PSALM 111:2

As I walk through the woods and pause to consider the unique design of the Red Trillium, I am filled with delight! To take in such a masterpiece of God's infinite creativity fills me with wonder. My heart responds in humility and thankfulness.

Make God the utmost delight and pleasure of your life, and
He will provide for you what you desire most.

PSALM 37:4 TPT

I delight in experiencing the beauty God has placed all around me, but my greater delight is in the One who created me from the overflow of His love! He longs to draw near and meet the desires of my heart.

Thank you, Lord, for creating my inmost being and for placing deep desires in my heart that You love to fill so that I might come to experience my greatest delight—the JOY of knowing You!

—a feeling of surprise mixed with admiration; a response to something beautiful, unexpected or unfamiliar

The Jack-In-The-Pulpit brings an unexpected sense of wonder to the woodland floor. Like an image from a fairy tale, our hero Jack stands tall in the "pulpit," partially shrouded by a festive green and maroon striped, stylishly tapered hood. Completing the scene is an entourage of lush green leaves which encircle the bloom.

Take a good look at God's wonders—they'll take your breath away.

PSALM 66:5 MSG

Wonder is evoked by something we behold with our senses—something beautiful, unexpected, or unfamiliar. But, in Scripture, a "wonder" also refers to a special display of God's power and creativity. It is a gift from God that stirs deep in our hearts. It is a heart awakened to the treasures that fill us with awe and gratitude. It is a heart that knows God is the source of everything good and beautiful in our lives.

Go ahead and give God thanks for all the glorious things He has done!
Go ahead and worship Him! Tell everyone about His wonders!

PSALM 105:1 TPT

Lord, my heart is overflowing with worship and praise because of the world of wonder You have placed all around me! I will not stay silent; I will sing of Your marvelous works! You fill me with JOY!

purpose

—the reason for which someone or something exists; the intention or objective given by a creator.

Iris season is one of my favorite times of the year! Its blossoms are like true royalty among the kingdom of spring perennials. Each flower's intricate design, exquisite form, and vibrant color are nothing short of sublime. And the procession of blooms in an iris garden can last for an entire month. This subtle but charming yellow, two-toned iris is one of the first to arrive—and point us back to its Creator.

We look at this Son and see the God who cannot be seen. We look at this Son and see God's original purpose in everything created. For everything, absolutely everything … got started in Him and finds its purpose in Him.

COLOSSIANS 1:15-16 MSG

When I am reminded that "everything got started in Him and finds its purpose in Him," I imagine how Jesus delights in the beauty of every single iris petal He has created—and how much more He delighted in creating me! He has created each of His sons and daughters for a special purpose. We find our true value, meaning, and purpose in Him.

Lord, when life gets confusing, I know to always come back to You. I will trust in You alone. Your ways are higher than mine—and You are always good! Thank You for creating me with a unique plan and purpose. I know that in it, I will find You and the path of abundant life. Thank You for loving me.

surpass

—to go beyond anything good; to be better than what is expected or hoped for; to exceed.

This brilliant purple iris is a wonder to behold. Its elegant form and the depth of its color surpass mere words. Shifting rich hues and shimmering iridescence are brought out in the petals as the sun moves across the sky. As I gaze upon this masterpiece, my attention turns to the Designer, and my heart responds in gratitude. What a privilege to witness the work of His hands!

His unforgettable works of surpassing wonder reveal His grace and tender mercy.

PSALM 111:4

I pray that you, being rooted and established in love, may have power, together with all the Lord's holy people, to grasp how wide and long and high and deep is the love of Christ, and to know this love that surpasses knowledge ...

EPHESIANS 3:17B-19A

God Himself is the supreme example of why "surpass" is part of our vocabulary. Not only do all His works "go beyond anything good," but His very nature is better than anything we could have expected or hoped for. In God's attribute of love, we find a depth that surpasses all understanding—but is always available for us to experience and dive in deeper.

Lord, I am filled with awe as I come into Your presence. Everything about You stretches and exceeds my imagination. My heart's desire is to experience new depths of Your love, which surpasses anything I have known. I long to behold Your goodness and glory.

splendor

—brilliant distinction; grandeur; magnificence; glory.

Splendor is not a word that comes up in everyday conversation, but I cannot think of a more fitting way to describe this magnificent blossom. With mottled lavender petals on a backdrop of deep burgundy, this iris evokes an air of grandeur. And yet, its majestic blooms completely pale in comparison to the splendor of our King.

Everything I am will praise and bless the Lord! O Lord, my God, Your greatness takes my breath away, overwhelming me by Your majesty, beauty, and splendor!

PSALM 104:1 TPT

Let them praise the name of the Lord, for His name alone is exalted; His splendor is above the earth and the heavens.

PSALM 148:13

A prayer of declaration adapted from Psalm 145:3-7:

Lord, You are worthy of all of my praise. No one can fathom Your greatness. I will tell of Your mighty acts and speak of the glorious splendor of Your majesty. I will meditate on Your wonderful works. I will celebrate your abundant goodness and joyfully sing of Your righteousness. Let everything that has breath praise the Lord!

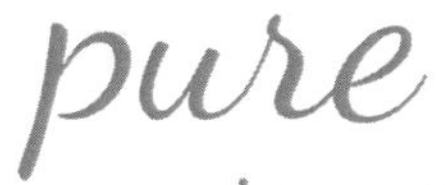

—immaculate; unstained; blameless; true.

The first time I walked through an Iris garden, it was the vibrant array of colors that grabbed my attention! But then, my gaze was drawn to the immaculate beauty and nobility of the white Irises, which seemed to stand out from all the rest. Their shining white brilliance provides a vivid picture of purity and all it represents.

Create in me a pure heart, O God, and renew a steadfast spirit within me.

PSALM 51:10

The Old Testament is filled with compelling illustrations of the power of sin and our need for a Savior. Now through Jesus' shed blood on the cross, we may receive the righteousness of Christ and be made as white as snow. But, to remain blameless and in close fellowship with the Lord, we need to confess our sins—removing all our guilt and shame.

Blessed are the pure in heart, for they will see God.

MATTHEW 5:8

Another part of purity is to have a heart that is true. We were born with a desire to see the face of God. When we seek to live as people of one thing—pursuing God with single-mindedness and trusting in Him alone—we start to perceive His presence and glory with greater clarity. And one day, we will see Him face-to-face.

Who may ascend the mountain of the Lord? Who may stand in his holy place? The one who has clean hands and a pure heart …

PSALM 24:3-4A

Lord, thank You for the brilliant displays of purity we find in nature. In them we find greater understanding of deep spiritual truths. Fill me with pure thoughts and holy desires so that I might know Your heart and see You more clearly.

16

—relating to a king or queen; noble; majestic; stately.

This regal iris commands attention in any flower garden. Its velvet burgundy petals, lavish accents, and stately manner create an air of royalty as it holds court. God, the Master Artisan, captivates us with this noble blossom. It gives us but a glimpse into the majesty of the King of kings and Lord of lords.

Look! Yahweh now reigns as King! He has covered Himself with majesty and strength, wearing them as His splendor-garments. Regal power surrounds Him as He sits securely on His throne …

PSALM 93:1 TPT

Sometimes we can get caught up in the chaos and uncertainty of the world and begin to lose our footing. It is good to be reminded, "The Lord reigns, He is robed in majesty, He is armed with strength, He is mighty, and the world is firmly established; it cannot be moved."

PSALM 93:1 NIV

Lord, sometimes I have a tendency to try to crawl back up on the throne of my life and take control, but that is not a crown I was meant to wear. I desire for You alone to be Lord and King of my life. You rule with wisdom and regal power—and You are always GOOD. I stand in awe of You.

extravagant

—exceeding the limits of reason or necessity; outrageous, lavish, beyond generous.

I will never forget the first time I discovered this brilliant blue and yellow iris and how I was wowed by its striking color. Then as I drew closer to take it all in, I was astounded to find the blue petals were etched in gold! Its stunning beauty and lavish accents were beyond anything I had imagined—an extravagant display of God's artistry!

Our world and all of eternity will never be the same because Jesus exceeded the limits of all reason—giving His life to save us. His love is truly extravagant. And now, we are called to love others lavishly, just as Christ loved us and gave of Himself sacrificially.

Watch what God does, and then you do it, like children who learn proper behavior from their parents. Mostly what God does is love you.

EPHESIANS 5:1 MSG

Keep company with Him and learn a life of love. Observe how Christ loved us. His love was not cautious but extravagant. He didn't love in order to get something from us but to give everything of Himself to us. Love like that.

EPHESIANS 5:2 MSG

Lord, You have exceeded the limits of reason; the way You love is outrageous, lavish, and goes beyond all generosity. We give You all the praise, honor, and glory! Thank You for showing us new depths of extravagant love. It is our highest calling—to love like You.

grow

—to increase, to spring up, and develop to maturity.

An iris garden begins with tender shoots that emerge under the right soil conditions. Then, as the roots become well established, the plants increase in size and strength until they develop sturdy stems with lovely buds. With the necessary amount of sunshine and moisture, changes can be seen daily until the graceful blooms emerge. Watching plants grow and reach maturity reminds us that there is a beauty and a rhythm to every living thing that God has created.

Our world is filled with evidence of growth. We instinctively know it is a sign of health and vitality. Part of what defines life itself is the "capacity for growth and change." God created the desire in each of us to grow and transform until we are fully mature. Deep down, we know that we cannot stay the same. Much like a good earthly father, our heavenly Father wants us to mature and reach our full potential. That is when we will blossom and become the most fruitful.

God wants us to grow up, to know the whole truth, and tell it in love—like Christ in everything. We take our lead from Christ, who is the source of everything we do. He keeps us in step with each other. His very breath and blood flow through us, nourishing us so that we will grow up healthy in God, robust in love.

EPHESIANS 4:15-16 MSG

Grow in grace and understanding of our Master and Savior, Jesus Christ. Glory to the Master, now and forever! Yes!

2 PETER 3:18 MSG

Thank You, Lord, that our growth and maturity are filled with great purpose. You are the source of life—and it is when we are rooted and established in Your Word that we grow and thrive. Grow us in grace and understanding until we learn to live a life of ever-increasing faith, hope, and love.

19

kindness

—sensitive to the needs of others; the quality of being considerate; a sincere desire for the happiness and well-being of others.

By mid-June, the sun-loving Blanket Flowers are in full bloom. They can cover an entire area with festive red, yellow, and orange blossoms—resembling a gathering of playful sunflowers. These hardy perennials tirelessly produce blooms that attract bees and butterflies throughout the growing season. I see God's kindness in these delightful flowers. He is so generous and considerate in creating beauty that continually brings us joy.

Lord, how wonderfully You bless the righteous. Your favor wraps around each one and covers them under Your canopy of kindness and joy.

PSALM 5:12 TPT

I love the picture this Scripture paints. What a beautiful image—to be fully covered by a canopy of God's kindness and joy. Our Creator is so gracious and considerate that it melts my heart. Here is another Bible passage that goes on to describe the full expression of God's kindness to us in His Son:

But because of His great love for us, God, who is rich in mercy, made us alive with Christ even when we were dead in transgressions—it is by grace you have been saved. And God raised us up with Christ and seated us with Him in the heavenly realms in Christ Jesus, in order that in the coming ages He might show the incomparable riches of His grace, expressed in His kindness to us in Christ Jesus.

EPHESIANS 2:4-7 NIV

Thank You, Lord, for Your unlimited loving-kindness. I am forever grateful. Fashion my heart to be a funnel of Your grace.

20

—to search for; to be intent on; to pursue after.

Watching bees bustling with activity in a Blanket Flower garden is fascinating. They appear to be on a mission as they search for blossoms with sweet nectar. Even close-up photography rarely interrupts their quest for the prize. It doesn't take long to discover how well God designed bees to seek out the nourishment they need to thrive. Another notable part of their design is how pollen clings to specialized hairs on their body as they gather nectar. So, as they pursue after what sustains them, bees spread pollen to other flowers—which produces new life and fruitfulness.

You will seek Me and find Me when you seek Me with all of your heart.

JEREMIAH 29:13

Scripture is clear that we are designed to seek God—and for good reason. Acts 17:24 declares:

"The God who made the world and everything in it is the Lord of Heaven and earth ... He Himself gives all men life and breath and everything else."

Sometimes we need to be reminded of who God is and all He has done for us. He is the very source of our life and everything good in it. And the fact that the Creator of the universe invites us to seek Him and have a deep relationship with Him seems unfathomable!

To seek God requires a humble and surrendered heart. It is from that place we begin to hear His voice and encounter His nature and character. The wonderful promise to those who seek Him is that He will be found. To experience God's presence is what we were made for! Nothing else truly satisfies.

Lord, thank You for the sweet delight of knowing You. Your Word is like honey to my soul. As I regularly seek Your face, make me a "carrier" of the righteousness, peace, and joy of heaven—so that I might spread great hope to the world around me!

21

—a profound feeling of wonder mixed with reverence, admiration, or fear—typically produced by something (beautiful, powerful, or dreadful) that overwhelms the senses.

In the stillness of an early summer morning, daylight begins to awaken the dawn. In a moment, the muted tones of the sky break forth into an array of color. The silhouettes of Daisies stand tall against the backdrop of a radiant sunrise… And I stand in awe. The privilege of witnessing such a display of God's glory and majesty is overwhelming. I watch the scene unfold with my eyes, but more deeply, I sense God's presence in my heart. In humility and reverence, I thank Him for His beautiful gifts that fill me with wonder.

O God, to the farthest corners of the planet, people will stand in awe, startled and stunned by Your signs and wonders. Sunrise brilliance and sunset beauty both take turns singing their songs of joy to You.

PSALM 65:8 TPT

When I gaze upon the beauty of the rising sun, I am amazed to ponder that the One who calls forth the dawn knows me and calls me by name. When I observe how the sunset ushers in the night, I am reminded of the brilliant rhythms God has established on the earth—and how we are invited to join in the joyous dance over all creation.

This is the day the Lord has made; let us rejoice and be glad in it.

PSALM 118:24

"The Lord God Most High is astonishing, awesome beyond words! He's the formidable and powerful King over all the earth."

PSALM 47:2 TPT

22

Oh, Sovereign Lord, I am filled with awe and wonder as I come into Your presence. And I am overwhelmed by Your glory as I humbly bow before your throne. You alone are worthy of my worship and praise. Let everything that has breath praise the Lord!

light

—waves of energy that illuminate and overtake the darkness; the spectrum that makes vision possible—bringing colors to life.

God has been "lighting up the darkness" since the beginning. He spoke into the formless void, and light burst forth. Now we get to see! Our world is illuminated with perpetual beauty on display—like this bright and shining Daisy garden at dawn. Light plays an essential role in how we perceive the world with our eyes. With shifting light and shadows, even a garden of flowers can produce countless scenes as the sun arcs across the sky.

It started when God said, "Light up the darkness!" And our lives filled up with light as we saw and understood God in the face of Christ, all bright and beautiful.

2 CORINTHIANS 4:6 MSG

The depth and meaning of how light is described in Scripture is brilliant. When God caused His light to shine in our hearts, the knowledge of His glory was revealed in the face of the Son! Now, not only do we see with our eyes, but our hearts are flooded with light. Jesus truly is the way, the truth, and the life. He alone lights the way to salvation. That is good news!

"I am the light of the world. Whoever follows Me will never walk in darkness, but will have the light of life."

JOHN 8:12

To all who received Him, to those who believed in His name, He gave the right to become children of God.

JOHN 1:12

Thank You, Lord, for calling forth the light that allows us to see the beauty of creation all around us with our own eyes. Thank You for the light of Your revelation that allows us to see into the spiritual realm with the eyes of our heart. Jesus, You are the light of life!

23

generous

—a willingness to give beyond what is expected; a desire to share abundantly; to serve from a kind and noble heart.

These brilliant white daisies stand out against a striking background of gold and scarlet blossoms! When I gaze upon flowers in such a lavish display of color, I reflect on God's generous gifts and how He loves to delight our senses. Witnessing such beauty is refreshing to the soul and stirs up joy! In nature, God has given us an abundance of pictures that provide glimpses into His magnificent glory.

The Lord God is brighter than the brilliance of a sunrise! Wrapping Himself around me like a shield, He is so generous with His gifts of grace and glory. Those who walk along His paths with integrity will never lack one thing they need, for He provides it all!

PSALM 84:11 TPT

Sometimes our thoughts become narrow and filled with the tasks of everyday living—forgetting that God provides us with everything we need. You may not have access to a garden of Daisies to remind you of God's great generosity, so instead, step outside and look into the heavens, quietly sit in awe on a starry night, or immerse yourself in the surround sound of the great outdoors. Reminders of our generous God are all around us. We just need fresh eyes to see.

Jesus declared, "I have come to give you everything in abundance, more than you expect—life in its fullness until you overflow!"

JOHN 10:10 TPT

[Lord,] when you open Your generous hand, it's full of blessings, satisfying the longings of every living thing.

PSALM 145:16 TPT

24

Father, You are the kindest and most generous being in the universe. May I never forget that even life itself is an amazing gift from You. The abundance of Your grace overflows in every area of my life, and my heart is filled with gratitude.

strength

—power; might; the quality of being physically, mentally, or spiritually strong; the capacity to withstand great force or to resist pressure.

A summer thunderstorm rolled through with a blast of wind and a pounding rain. I fully expected to find the daisy garden riddled and beaten down by the storm. Though saturated by the heavy rain, the blossoms stood tall, and they seemed even more beautiful as they glistened in the sun. God designed the flora all around us to be amazingly resilient to the forces of nature, and to ultimately thrive through challenging conditions.

So, here's what I've learned through it all: Leave all your cares and anxieties at the feet of the Lord, and measureless grace will strengthen you.

PSALM 55:22 TPT

God's glory is all around me! His wrap-around presence is all I need, for the Lord is my Savior, my hero, and my life-giving strength.

PSALM 62:7 TPT

Sometimes the storms of life seem like more than we can bear. Yet, God never intended for us to go it alone, or to rely on our own strength to get through every trial. It is when we are pushed beyond our own power and endurance that we discover what the Lord revealed to Paul:

"My grace is sufficient for you, for my power is made perfect in weakness." Therefore, I will boast all the more gladly about my weaknesses, so that Christ's power may rest on me … For when I am weak, then I am strong.

2 CORINTHIANS 12:9-10

This is my prayer:

Lord, you are my true strength and my glory-song, my champion, my Savior!

PSALM 118:14 TPT

—having desires fulfilled; made content; to please someone by giving them what they need.

To bask in the glory of a sunrise over this garden of daisies brings refreshment to my soul. The Lord used a pastel pallet to paint the morning sky, and the color is softly reflected in the daisy blossoms, which seem poised to greet the dawn. The beauty has captured my full attention, and my only response is to be still and know. I am filled with wonder and deep contentment because I know God created this moment for me to enjoy! I am fully satisfied.

The Lord will guide you always; He will satisfy your needs in a sun-scorched land and will strengthen your frame. You will be like a well-watered garden, like a spring whose waters never fail.

ISAIAH 58:11 NIV

To know You is to experience a flowing fountain, drinking in Your life, springing up to satisfy …

PSALM 36:9 TPT

Healthy gardens are full of life, growth, and fruitfulness. Yet, if plants lose their water supply, it doesn't take long for them to wither and become scorched in the heat of the sun. When you are in Christ, it is like being planted by an endless spring of living water. God refreshes your inmost being and satisfies the desires of your heart. He is the author and sustainer of an abundant and satisfying life!

I am convinced that my God will fully satisfy every need you have, for I have seen the abundant riches of glory revealed to me through Jesus Christ!

PHILIPPIANS 4:19 TPT

Lord, You alone fulfill the deepest desires of my heart. You satisfy my soul with your LOVE.

—to cease all activity in order to relax, refresh and recover strength; a period of stillness and calm; to fully trust, to wait confidently.

What a delight it is to come upon a fawn quietly resting in the Clover, waiting on its mother's return. After observing this young deer for a few hours, I started to become more concerned, wondering if its mother was close by and if she would be back. I have since learned that the mother of a newborn fawn may be gone for several hours at a time. But God has designed young fawns to be still, rest, and wait confidently for her.

From the beginning, the God of the universe, the maker of heaven and earth, designed rest to be an essential part of the rhythm of life. We need designated times when we can "hit pause," cease striving, refresh, and renew our trust in Him. There may be periods when we resist the need to recharge, but our body, soul, and spirit all require it. We grow and thrive from a place of rest.

Find rest, O my soul, in God alone; my hope comes from Him.

PSALM 62:5

The rest described in Scripture goes beyond ceasing from work and recovering strength. It is a quiet confidence that comes from deeply trusting in the nature and character of God. When we carve out time to find our resting place in the Lord, we discover the great security and unparalleled peace we enjoy in Him alone.

Whoever dwells in the shelter of the Most High will rest in the shadow of the Almighty. I will say of the Lord, "He is my refuge and my fortress, my God, in whom I trust."

PSALM 91:1-2

In a quiet time, allow these words from the Lord to wash over your soul:

"Are you tired? Worn out? Burned out on religion? Come to me. Get away with Me, and you'll recover your life. I'll show you how to take a real rest."

MATTHEW 11:28 MSG

27

—to rely upon or place confidence in someone or something; to believe in.

This whimsical flower is called Wild Bergamot. Its lavender pompoms can be found dancing gleefully in the breeze. Bees congregate to gather nectar from the blossoms at most any time of day. Not surprisingly, this late summer bloom is also called Bee Balm because of its prized nectar!

Taking time to appreciate these plants and insects helps me to recognize God's goodness and faithfulness in how He has designed every living thing. And although there is much I do not understand, my mind can fully rest in His nature and His ways.

All God accomplishes is flawless, faithful, and fair, and His every word proves trustworthy and true.

PSALM 111:7 TPT

For God's Word is something to sing about! He is true to His promises, His word can be trusted, and everything He does is reliable and right.

PSALM 33:4. TPT

A great truth found in God's Word is that He is completely trustworthy. There is nothing and no one in all the universe more worthy of our full confidence. When we come to a place of wholehearted and unwavering trust in Him, God gives us abiding peace and abundant hope.

You will keep in perfect peace him whose mind is steadfast because he trusts in You. Trust in the Lord forever, for the Lord, the Lord, is the Rock eternal.

ISAIAH 26:3-4

Lord, you are "The hope that holds me and the Stronghold to shelter me ... My great confidence" (Psalm 91:2 TPT). We declare, "Yes, and AMEN!"

28

—the core of who you are; your innermost being; the seat of affection.

The Coneflower is a classic perennial, seen here with vibrant pink, lavender, and white petals that gracefully bow around its central cone. It is a hardy flower that attracts a variety of bees and butterflies to its nectar. Later in the season, the cone forms a cluster of seeds that become a natural bird feeder for finches, cardinals, and jays. What a beautiful picture that God created the heart of the Coneflower to be a life-sustaining source.

Above all, guard the affections of your heart … Pay attention to the welfare of your innermost being, for from there flows the wellspring of life.

PROVERBS 4:23 TPT

God designed our hearts to be deeply rich and overflowing with life. It is vitally important that we pay attention to the condition of our heart—focusing on all that brings life, hope, strength, and refreshment to the very core of our being.

Delight yourself in the Lord, and He will give you the desires of your heart.

PSALM 37:4 NIV

The Lord Himself loves to fill the deep desires of our heart. He is the most loving, kind, compassionate, generous, joyful, peaceful, beautiful, and faithful being in the universe. He is Abba, Father—the author of life! Spend time with Him; He is the living Word. Give Him all of your honor and praise. And as you delight in Him, you will discover how much He delights in you. He rejoices over you with singing! He treasures your inmost being.

With my whole heart, with my whole life, and with my innermost being, I bow in wonder and love before you, the holy God!

PSALM 103:1 TPT

I give you thanks, oh Lord.

—deep affection, to delight in, to cherish, and to honor.

The tranquil beauty of the Coneflower at sunset is captivating. The subtle shades of each pink petal are enhanced by the soft light, bringing its lovely form to life. To be fully present and behold this scene is a gift. I delight in how God creates beauty out of love for me. He shows His love in a thousand different ways—and when we embrace it, we are filled beyond measure. Nothing compares to experiencing God's love!

Let everyone give all their praise and thanks to the Lord! Here's why—He's better than anyone could ever imagine. Yes, He's always loving and kind, and His faithful love never ends.

PSALM 107:1 TPT

The most meaningful thing we can do on our journey of faith is to abide in God's love. The descriptors of His love in Scripture are amazing and unfathomable. God's love is extravagant, faithful, and unending. He is passionate about His bride. There is nothing better than His love!

May the resting place of Christ's love become the very source and root of your life. Then you will discover the great magnitude of His love in all its dimensions—endless love beyond measure that fills you to overflowing with the goodness of God.

EPHESIANS 3:17-19 (PARAPHRASED)

God created our hearts to receive His love. He is the Beautiful One who fills us and completes us in every way. Make this declaration over your life today:

I am like a flourishing olive tree, anointed in the house of God. I trust in the unending love of God; His passion toward me is forever and ever.

PSALM 52:8 TPT

—to grasp the meaning of; to perceive; to comprehend.

To encounter a fawn in nature is always a delight! This one's beautiful eyes, delicate features, and speckled coat captured my attention. I could tell by its inquisitive posture that I had its full attention as well. I was surprised at how close I was able to approach. The curiosity of youth seemed to override its fear of the unfamiliar. Of course, a fawn's understanding is limited, but God designed all of His creatures with an instinct for self-preservation.

God looks down from heaven on all mankind to see if there are any who understand, any who seek God.

PSALM 53:2

We were all created with a deep desire to know God. But, it is when we turn aside to seek Him that we begin a life-long journey to comprehend the nature, character, and amazing love of our Father.

Open up my understanding to the ways of Your wisdom, and I will meditate deeply on Your splendor and Your wonders.

PSALM 119:27 TPT

"Let not the wise boast of their wisdom or the strong boast of their strength or the rich boast of their riches, but let the one who boasts boast about this: that they understand and know Me, that I am the Lord, who exercises kindness, justice, and righteousness on the earth, for in these I delight," declares the Lord.

JEREMIAH 9:23-24

Holy Spirit, my heart's desire is to know You and understand You more. I long to encounter Your goodness in a way that brings me to an experiential knowledge of Your kindness, justice, and righteousness. You are my delight—I will boast in You alone!

31

transformation

—a significant change in appearance or character; metamorphosis.

There is something captivating to all ages about observing the graceful flight of a butterfly. This tiger swallowtail was fluttering about before finding sweet nectar in the marigold garden. Its bold striped wings, trimmed with orange and metallic blue highlights, are striking. The life cycle of a butterfly is fascinating, and it is one of the most astounding examples of metamorphosis in nature. Though far less apparent to a casual observer, the inner transformation that begins in a new believer is even more profound and beautiful.

If anyone is in Christ, he is a new creation; the old has gone, the new has come!

2 CORINTHIANS 5:17

Be transformed as you embrace the glorious Christ-within as your new life and live in union with Him! For God has recreated you all over again in His perfect righteousness, and you now belong to Him in the realm of true holiness.

EPHESIANS 4:24 TPT

What a gift it is to be transformed in the attitude of our minds. It is unfathomable how God created us anew—to be like Him in righteousness and holiness—that is good news! Our part is to live in union with Christ; God is the one who changes us from the inside out.

Stop imitating the ideals and opinions of the culture around you, but be inwardly transformed by the Holy Spirit through a total reformation of how you think. This will empower you to discern God's will as you live a beautiful life, satisfying and perfect in his eyes.

ROMANS 12:2 TPT

32

The Holy Spirit has the most joyful job in the universe. He oversees every aspect of our transformation as we are conformed to the image of Christ! And it is with the renewing of our minds that we learn to discern God's will—to walk in His ways and experience the abundant life.

You have acquired new creation life, which is continually being renewed into the likeness of the One who created you; giving you the full revelation of God.

COLOSSIANS 3:10 TPT

goodness

—loving-kindness; focused on the benefit of others; upright in heart and character.

Whether in mid-flight or peacefully spreading its wings, a Monarch butterfly is a wonder to behold. Its vibrant orange wings, trimmed in black with white highlights, bring a touch of royalty to any garden. One of the most fascinating facts about the Monarch is that during migration, it may travel up to 3,000 miles—often logging around 100 miles each day! When I take in its beauty and ponder its migratory feats, I think of God's brilliance and His goodness in all that He has created on the earth.

For the Lord is always good and ready to receive you. He's so loving that it will amaze you—so kind that it will astound you! And He is famous for His faithfulness toward all. Everyone knows our God can be trusted, for He keeps His promises to every generation!

PSALM 100:5 TPT

Reading and meditating on this Psalm is a great way to awaken the senses to the goodness of the Father in every area of your life. God wants to give you a higher vision and refined focus for how He views this world. As you spend time renewing your mind in the truth of His goodness, you will begin to see more clearly.

God, everyone sees Your goodness, for Your tender love is blended into everything You do.

PSALM 145:9 TPT

Everything You do is beautiful, flowing from Your goodness;
teach me the power of Your wonderful words!

PSALM 119:68 TPT

Thank You, Lord, that Your goodness is at the very essence of Your glory! Spirit of wisdom and revelation, open the eyes of my heart to see Your infinite goodness in all things.

33

—quietness of mind; tranquility; to be in harmony.

There are times when God paints on the canvas of nature in order to place one of His attributes on display. To watch a Clouded Yellow Butterfly glide about the garden on a still summer day, then dine on nectar from the lovely Zinnias, that is a picture of peace. The tranquility of the scene is a masterpiece that quiets the soul. And yet, the peace of God, which transcends all understanding, exceeds the serenity that any image can capture.

Let the peace of Christ rule in your hearts, since as members of one body, you were called to peace ...

COLOSSIANS 3:15

It is hard to wrap our minds around peace being the "ruler" of anything. In Greek, this phrase literally means, "Let peace be the umpire of your minds." When you allow the peace of Christ to rule in your heart, it won't allow anything to enter or remain that is not in harmony with His perfect peace.

Everything I've taught you is so that the peace which is in Me will be in you and will give you great confidence as you rest in Me.

JOHN 16:33 TPT

Deep peace comes from trusting in Jesus and resting in the victory He has already secured. It is what our hearts long for—to walk in assurance and to become unshakable in our confidence.

Do not be anxious about anything, but in everything, by prayer and petition, with thanksgiving, present your requests to God. And the peace of God, which transcends all understanding, will guard your hearts and your minds in Christ Jesus.

PHILIPPIANS 4:6-7

fruit

—loving-kindness; focused on the benefit of others; upright in heart and character.

I am captivated by sunflowers. Their regal golden-yellow petals radiate from each seed-filled center. As the sun moves across the sky, the blossoms actually turn to bask in its glory. What a beautiful metaphor for how we have the opportunity each day to seek the face of the Son and rest in the radiance of His presence. Sunflowers not only provide late summer beauty, but they also produce nourishment for bees, butterflies, birds, and people. In fact, a single sunflower may yield up to 2,000 seeds. What amazing fruit!

God created us to produce good and abundant fruit as well. The fruit of the Holy Spirit is a result of abiding in Christ and being transformed by the Spirit. Becoming fruitful is more than just a good theory. Jesus beautifully demonstrated the fruit that is possible when we walk in the Spirit. When we remain in Him, our capacity to bear fruit is limitless!

But the fruit produced by the Holy Spirit within you is divine love in all its varied expressions: joy that overflows, peace that subdues, patience that endures, kindness in action, a life full of virtue, faith that prevails, gentleness of heart, and strength of spirit. Never set the law above these qualities, for they are meant to be limitless.

GALATIANS 5:22-23 TPT

Blessed is the one... whose delight is in the law of the Lord, and who meditates on his law day and night. That person is like a tree planted by streams of water, which yields its fruit in season and whose leaf does not wither—whatever they do prospers.

PSALM 1:1-3 NIV (ADAPTED)

Lord, like your most pleasing Sunflower, I desire to turn to You and seek Your glory and grace each day. I long to meditate on your Word and follow your ways! May my life become continually fruitful as I follow after You.

35

—free from sin; blameless; to walk in justice and truth.

What a delightful gift to discover the Autumn Crocus on a walk through the park in late September! While most flowering plants have already withered, its vivid lavender blooms provide a splash of color to the earthen tones of fall. Surprisingly, the Autumn Crocus is not a Crocus after all; it is a member of the Lily family. This unexpected fall blossom was just right in God's eyes—bringing a touch of beauty to the changing season.

The Lord is righteous in all His ways and loving toward all He has made.

PSALM 145:17

The fruit of the righteous is a tree of life …

PROVERBS 11:30A

The God who fashioned a blooming treasure to arrive at harvest time cares about every detail of His creation. The order of the universe and the laws of nature all come into alignment with His righteousness. It is a compelling expression of God's holiness, and what sets Him apart.

Your righteousness reaches to the skies, O God, You who have done great things. Who, O God is like You?

PSALM 71:19

Above all, constantly seek God's Kingdom and His righteousness …

MATTHEW 6:33A TPT

36

Lord, You are just and true and good in all of Your ways. Who is like You? Everything You say and do comes under the glorious and vast umbrella of Your righteousness. You are perfect in holiness. I will give You all of the glory and honor and praise!

steadfast

—immovable, firmly fixed; loyal, unwavering in belief and commitment.

Although the Park Woodland is full of ever-changing beauty, the trees themselves are a natural picture of steadfastness. The way God designed trees is fascinating. A healthy tree is able to withstand intense storms and the challenging conditions of every season. The secret to a thriving tree is the quality and strength of its root system hidden underground. Amazingly, it serves as both an anchor of stability and a lifeline for taking in water and nutrients—allowing the tree to grow and thrive.

The steadfast nature of God is unparalleled. He is our firm foundation. He is our solid Rock.

The steadfast love of the Lord never ceases, His mercies never come to an end; they are new every morning; great is Your faithfulness.

LAMENTATIONS 3:22-23

You will keep in perfect peace those whose minds are steadfast because they trust in You. Trust in the Lord forever, for the Lord Himself is the Rock eternal.

ISAIAH 26:3-4

Much like trees, the strength of your life will be determined by your root system. Are you firmly rooted in the Word? In the secret place, are you growing deep in your faith and intimacy with the Lord? When a storm blows through, whatever is anchored in Christ cannot be shaken. Trusting in the goodness, faithfulness, and love of God is the steadfast root that will keep you in perfect peace—no matter what circumstances you face.

So then, just as you received Christ Jesus as Lord, continue to live in Him, rooted and built up in Him, strengthened in the faith ... and overflowing with thankfulness.

COLOSSIANS 2:6

faithfulness

—devotion; to be trustworthy, loyal, and dependable.

It's mid-October in Iowa, and blooms can still be found in the Blanket Flower garden. Even though their full brilliance has faded, the contrast of the late-season blossoms and the dried seed heads offer a unique blend of beauty and imperfection. I was pleased to capture the dainty Eastern Tailed-Blue butterfly drawing nourishment from the dwindling supply of nectar. God's faithfulness is so evident in His tender care for every living thing.

You are the Lord who reigns over your never-ending kingdom through all the ages of time and eternity! You are faithful to fulfill every promise You've made.

PSALM 145:13 TPT

Praise the Lord, all you nations; extol Him, all you peoples. For great is His love towards us, and the faithfulness of the Lord endures forever.

PSALM 117:1-2

In this we can place our full confidence, God's faithfulness is never-ending. He is our living HOPE. Our security does not rest on earthly things, but on the promises of God—on His great love, kindness, and faithfulness.

Keep trusting in the Lord and do what is right in His eyes. Fix your heart on the promises of God and you will be secure, feasting on His faithfulness.

PSALM 37:3 TPT

At each and every sunrise, we will be thanking You for Your kindness and Your love. As the sun sets and all through the night, we will keep proclaiming, "You are so faithful!"

PSALM 92:2 TPT

38

thankfulness

—a heart of gratitude; filled with appreciation; well pleased.

Watching leaves transform from distinct shades of green to vibrant reds, yellows, and oranges is one of the great highlights of autumn! Although the fall colors peak for only a few weeks, and it's one of the first signs that winter is on its way, that does not distract from the magnificent color that can be seen in every direction. It is also a sign of harvest season and the bountiful blessings of the Lord. My heart wells up with thankfulness because I know the beauty of fall is another exquisite gift from our loving Heavenly Father.

With all my heart and passion I will thank You, my God! I will give glory to Your name, always and forever!

PSALM 86:12 TPT

I will give thanks to You, Lord, with all my heart; I will tell of all Your wonderful deeds. I will be glad and rejoice in You; I will sing the praises of Your name, O Most High.

PSALM 9:1-2

A thankful heart is a humble heart. It's a heart that recognizes God is the Creator of life, hope, love, and everything good. When we cultivate an attitude of thankfulness, it yields a life of peace, joy, and contentment. God's word is clear—we are to give thanks in all circumstances.

Let joy be your continual feast. Make your life a prayer. And in the midst of everything be always giving thanks, for this is God's perfect plan for you in Christ Jesus.

1 THESSALONIANS 5:16-19 TPT

Whatever you do, whether in word or deed, do it all in the name of the Lord Jesus, giving thanks to God the Father through Him.

COLOSSIANS 3:17

39

glory

—worthy of praise; brilliance, resplendence; magnificence, renown; exceptional beauty.

This crisp October morning is a showcase of all that I love about autumn! Gazing into a limitless azure sky on a clear day is a wonder in itself; but to combine that view with a magnificent green and yellow canopy of Maple trees in their prime is absolutely glorious. As light filters through the leaves, I am surrounded by a halo of gold. It's as if God encircled me with a glimpse of His glory. My only desire was to be still and bask in the resplendence of all that God has created. My heart is undone.

Keep your thoughts continually fixed on all that is authentic and real, honorable and admirable, beautiful and respectful, pure and holy, merciful and kind. And fasten your thoughts on every glorious work of God, praising Him always.

PHILIPPIANS 4:8 TPT

At the beginning of our devotional journey, we started with Philippians 4:8. This verse holds the key to renewing our minds—fixing our thoughts on good things. God has given us His Word and a world full of His goodness and beauty for those with eyes to see. The tall Maples, with their brilliant fall colors, are just one example of how God's infinite creativity is a display of His glory.

To truly grasp the magnitude of God's glory goes beyond our ability to perceive and understand. In one sense, it is to behold the radiance of His splendor. Yet, God's glory also encompasses attributes such as His goodness, His beauty, His honor, His greatness, and His holiness. As I meditate on God's divine qualities, I respond in stillness—filled with awe and wonder. This is our God, and our delight. Lord, there is none like You.

You are worthy, our Lord and God, to receive glory and honor and power, for You created all things, and by Your will they were created and have their being.

REVELATION 4:11

40

With my whole heart, with my whole life, and with my innermost being, I bow in wonder and love before You, the holy God!

PSALM 103:1 TPT

Our stroll through the park has come to an end. I hope you were blessed by our time together. My prayer is that you will continue on in your journey with the One who calls you by name.

> *"Come to me. Get away with me and recover your life. Walk with me and learn the unforced rhythms of grace. Keep company with me and discover the joy of living freely ..."*
>
> MATTHEW 11:28-30 MSG (PARAPHRASED)

Made in the USA
Monee, IL
05 May 2023